Cook it!

PaRragon

Bath • New York • Singapore • Hong Kong • Cologne • Delhi
Melbourne • Amsterdam • Johannesburg • Shenzhen

Cooking Things

Here's a list of the items of cooking equipment that you will need to make the recipes in this cookbook.

baking trays
balloon whisk
blender
muffin tin
cake tin
chopping board
colander

cooling rack
fish slice
flour shaker
food processor
frying pan
garlic crusher

grater
hand mixer
lemon squeezer
loaf tin

measuring jug
measuring spoons
mixing bowl
palette knife
pastry brush
rolling pin

round-bladed knife
round cutter
saucepans
scissors
sharp knife
sieve

slotted spoon
spatula
tongs
vegetable peeler

wooden skewers
wooden spoon

This edition published by Parragon in 2013
Parragon Books
Chartist House
15–17 Trim Street
Bath BA1 1HA, UK
www.parragon.com

ISBN 978-1-4723-1164-1

Printed in China

Using the recipes

The recipes in this book are graded with stars, meaning that some are more difficult than others:

★ = easy

★ ★ = a little tricky

★ ★ ★ = a little more challenging

The recipes also have symbols to help you. Look out for:

Serves/Makes

Preparation time

Cooking time

If you see the ❗ symbol, it means you need to ask an adult to help you. This could be because a hot oven, hob, electrical appliance, sharp knife or scissors are involved in the recipe preparation.

Safe cooking!

- Always ask an adult first before starting to cook and be especially careful when handling anything hot, sharp or electrical.
- Always wear oven gloves when handling hot baking trays, pans and dishes.
- When stirring food in a pan, hold the handle firmly to keep it steady.
- Turn pan handles to the side, away from the heat, so they aren't accidentally knocked off the hob.
- Remember to switch off the hob or oven when you have finished cooking.

Clean up

- Always wash your hands thoroughly before you start to cook and after handling raw meat and fish.
- Use separate chopping boards for vegetables and meat. If this is not possible, make sure they are washed thoroughly between uses.
- Store raw and cooked food separately in the fridge.
- Make sure that the ingredients you use have not passed their 'use-by' date.
- Wipe down work surfaces after use and make sure everything is clean and tidy.

Rate each recipe!

Cooking is all about fun, experimenting, learning and of course eating delicious food! At the end of each recipe there's a score box for your family and friends to give you marks out of 10 for your food, from a yummylicious 10 to an OK 1.

Breakfast Porridge★★

Just the thing to warm you up on a cold winter's morning, this creamy porridge is topped with a cinnamon apple puree, golden syrup and a sprinkling of pecan nuts.

Serves 4

Prep:
15 minutes

Cooking:
15 minutes

Equipment:

- vegetable peeler
- sharp knife
- chopping board
- fork
- small and large saucepans with lids
- large spoon

What you need:

275 g rolled oats

750 ml milk

750 ml water

8 pecan nuts, to serve (optional)

golden syrup, to serve

Cinnamon apple puree:

4 apples

1 tsp lemon juice

180 ml water

½–1 tsp ground cinnamon

Step 1: ⓘ

To make the puree, remove the skin from the apples, using a vegetable peeler. Cut the apple into quarters, remove the core, then cut the flesh into small pieces.

Step 2: ⓘ

Put the apple pieces, lemon juice, water and cinnamon in a small saucepan. Cover and simmer for 15 minutes, until the apples are soft.

Step 3: ⓘ

While the apple mixture is cooking, put the oats in a large saucepan with the milk and water, then bring to the boil.

Step 4: ⓘ

When the oat mixture is bubbling, reduce the heat to low; half cover the pan with a lid and simmer for 8 minutes, stirring frequently.

Step 5:

Mash the apple mixture with a fork until mushy. Spoon the creamy porridge into 4 bowls, then top each one with apple puree.

Step 6:

Add the pecans, if using, and drizzle over the golden syrup. Try arranging the nuts and syrup in a fun pattern, as shown on the opposite page.

Marks out of 10

10=yummylicious 9=truly scrumptious 8=de-lovely
7=delicious 6=tasty 5=Mmmmmmm
4=mouthwatering 3=just nice
2=good 1=ok

. . . .

5

Golden Nuggets **

This golden, crunchy breakfast cereal will give you plenty of energy. It's great served with milk or yogurt and topped with your favourite fresh fruit.

Makes about 10 portions

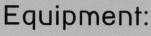

Cooking: 28 minutes

Prep: 15 minutes

Equipment:

- large mixing bowl
- wooden spoon
- small saucepan
- 2 baking trays

What you need:

100 g whole almonds, with skins removed

275 g rolled oats

50 g sesame seeds

50 g sunflower seeds

50 g pumpkin seeds

3 tbsp sunflower oil

8 tbsp honey

50 g shelled walnuts, roughly broken

100 g raisins

To serve:

your favourite fresh fruit, such as raspberries, sliced strawberries, bananas or nectarines milk or natural yogurt

Step 1: ⓘ
Turn the oven on to 275°F/140°C/gas mark 3. Put the almonds, oats and seeds in a large mixing bowl.

Step 2: ⓘ
Put the oil and honey in a small saucepan and, over a medium heat, stir until melted and mixed together.

Step 3: ⓘ
Pour the honey mixture into the mixing bowl and stir well with a wooden spoon, until the nuts, oats and seeds are coated.

Step 4: ⓘ
Spoon the oat mixture onto 2 baking trays in an even layer and bake for 15 minutes; then mix in the walnuts.

Step 5:
Bake the oat mixture for another 10 minutes, until golden. (The mixture will become crisp as it cools.)

Step 6:
Put the cereal in a mixing bowl and stir in the raisins. Allow to cool. Serve with milk or yogurt and top with fruit.

Marks out of 10
10=yummylicious 9=truly scrumptious 8=de-lovely
7=delicious 6=tasty 5=Mmmmmmm
4=mouthwatering 3=just nice
2=good 1=ok

. . . . ✓

Roll Up, Roll Up!★

This yummy roll is extra special because it has a secret layer of delicious pesto.

Makes 1

Prep:
10 minutes

Cooking:
none

Equipment:

- sharp knife
- chopping board
- spoon
- bowl
- cling film

What you need:

1 large crusty roll

1 tsp prepared green pesto

1 tbsp mayonnaise

2 slices ham or cooked chicken

2 crisp lettuce leaves

30 g cheese, cut into thin slices

4 thin, round slices cucumber

Step 1: !
Slice off the top of the roll to form a lid and use a spoon to scoop out the soft bread from the inside to make a hollow.

Step 2:
Mix together the pesto and mayonnaise in a bowl and spread it all over the inside of the roll and the lid.

Step 3:
Fold one of the slices of ham or chicken, then place it in the bottom of the roll. Top with the lettuce.

Step 4:
Next, add the remaining slice of ham or chicken and top with a layer of cheese.

Step 5:
Now add the cucumber, then press the filling down slightly and top with the roll lid.

Step 6:
The roll can be eaten straight away or wrapped in cling film and stored in the fridge for a few hours.

Marks out of 10
10=yummylicious 9=truly scrumptious 8=de-lovely
7=delicious 6=tasty 5=Mmmmmmm
4=mouthwatering 3=just nice
2=good 1=ok

. . . . ✔

9

Spicy Wraps★★★

These spicy wraps, called fajitas, taste sensational! They come from Mexico and are soft tortillas filled with meat, salad and some spicy sauce. You'll have a fab time making them!

Prep:
15 minutes
+ 1
hour
marinating

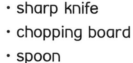

Cooking:
5-6 minutes

Makes 4

Equipment:

- sharp knife
- chopping board
- spoon
- bowl
- cling film
- frying pan

What you need:

1 red and 1 yellow pepper
2 skinless chicken breast fillets
2 tbsp olive oil
2 tsp mild chilli powder
1 tsp paprika
juice and grated rind of 1 lime
4 soft flour tortillas
55 g shredded iceberg lettuce
4 tbsp soured cream or plain yogurt

Spicy Tomato and Avocado Sauce:
2 tomatoes, deseeded and chopped
small red onion, very finely chopped
1 tbsp lime juice
1 tbsp olive oil
salt and freshly ground black pepper
1 avocado, peeled, stoned and diced
1 tbsp chopped fresh coriander

Step 1: ❗
Halve the peppers, remove the seeds and cut into long strips. Cut the chicken fillets into strips and place in a non-metallic dish.

Step 2:
Add half the oil, the spices and lime juice and rind. Mix together until the chicken is well coated. Cover with cling film and leave in the fridge for 1 hour.

Step 3:
To make the spicy tomato and avocado sauce, mix together all the ingredients. Add salt and pepper, cover and keep cool.

Step 4: ❗
Heat the remaining oil in a frying pan. Fry the chicken, stirring, for 3 minutes. Add the peppers and fry for 3 minutes, until the chicken is cooked.

Step 5: ❗
Remove pan from heat. Spoon out the chicken and peppers and keep warm. Heat the tortillas in the oven. Put the sauce and cream in bowls.

Step 6:
To make a fajita, put some sauce and sour cream onto a tortilla. Add the chicken, peppers and lettuce. Roll up the fajita and eat it!

Marks out of 10
10=yummylicious 9=truly scrumptious 8=de-lovely
7=delicious 6=tasty 5=Mmmmmmm
4=mouthwatering 3=just nice
2=good 1=ok

. . . . ✔

11

Crudités (sticks of raw vegetables) are fab finger food – great for lunch boxes, parties or just when you have the munchies! Chunky sticks of crisp vegetables with dreamy flavoured dips – mmmmm!

Serves 8

Prep:
45 minutes

Cooking:
none

Equipment:

- chopping board
- sharp knife
- mixing bowl
- wooden spoon
- food processor
- tablespoon
- serving plate
- 2 small bowls
- measuring jug

What you need:

Crudités:
4 carrots, peeled
2 courgettes
4 sticks of celery
half a cucumber
1 red pepper
1 yellow pepper
8 baby sweetcorn

Hummus:
400 g canned chickpeas, drained
juice of a lemon
2 cloves of garlic, crushed
2 tbsp tahini (sesame paste)
125 ml olive oil
salt and freshly ground black pepper
freshly chopped parsley and paprika to decorate

Cheesy dip:
250 g cream cheese
2 tbsp milk
2 spring onions, finely chopped
1 tbsp freshly chopped parsley
1 tbsp chives
salt and freshly ground black pepper

Step 1: ⚠️

Cut the carrots, courgettes and celery into sticks 6 cm long. Halve the cucumber, remove the seeds and cut into equal-sized sticks.

Step 2: ⚠️

Halve the peppers and remove the seeds. Cut each half into long strips.

Step 3:

Make the cheesy dip by mixing the cheese and milk until smooth. Add the other ingredients and season with salt and pepper.

Step 4: ⚠️

To make the hummus, blend the chickpeas, lemon juice and garlic in the processor. Add the tahini and blend until smooth.

Step 5: ⚠️

Keep the machine running and add the oil, a little at a time. Season with salt and pepper.

Step 6:

Put the dip and hummus in small bowls. Sprinkle the hummus with parsley and paprika. Put the bowls on a plate with the crudités around them.

Marks out of 10

10=yummylicious 9=truly scrumptious 8=de-lovely
7=delicious 6=tasty 5=Mmmmmmm
4=mouthwatering 3=just nice
2=good 1=ok

. . . . ✔

13

Sunset Soup ★★

You can use pumpkin instead of squash for this delicious and nutritious soup.

Serves 4

Prep:
15 minutes

Cooking:
30 minutes

Equipment:

- sharp knife
- chopping board
- large saucepan with lid
- spoon
- handheld electric blender
- ladle
- grater

What you need:

1 kg butternut squash
1 tbsp olive oil
1 large onion, sliced
1 celery stalk, sliced
1 leek, sliced
1 large carrot, sliced
1 litre vegetable stock
2 bay leaves
1 bouquet garni
1 tsp dried thyme
salt and freshly ground pepper
grated mature cheddar cheese
and crusty bread, to serve

Step 1: ⓘ

Cut the squash into thick slices, then cut off the skin. Scoop out the seeds with a spoon and cut into chunks.

Step 2: ⓘ

Heat the oil in a saucepan and fry the onion for 5 minutes, then add the squash, celery, leek and carrot; stir well.

Step 3: ⓘ

Cook the vegetables for 3 minutes with the lid on. Pour in the stock and add the bay leaves, bouquet garni and thyme.

Step 4: ⓘ

Bring the soup to a boil, then reduce the heat and simmer, half covered, for 20 minutes, until the vegetables are tender.

Step 5: ⓘ

Remove the pan from the heat and, using a handheld electric blender, blend the soup until smooth. Season with salt and pepper.

Step 6: ⓘ

Ladle the soup into bowls and top with a sprinkling of grated cheese. Serve with crusty bread.

Marks out of 10

10=yummylicious 9=truly scrumptious 8=de-lovely
7=delicious 6=tasty 5=Mmmmmmm
4=mouthwatering 3=just nice
2=good 1=ok

. . . . ✓

Salmon Bites★★

These golden, crispy balls of potato and brain-boosting salmon taste great and go well with the creamy dipping sauce.

Serves 4

Prep:
20 minutes,
plus chilling

Cooking:
25 minutes

Equipment:

- large mixing bowl
- grater
- spoon
- plate
- large frying pan
- spatula
- small mixing bowl
- paper towels

What you need:

2 x 213 g tins salmon, skin and large bones removed

630 g potatoes, peeled, cooked and cooled

1 small egg, beaten

flour, for coating

3 tbsp sunflower oil

salt and pepper

lemon wedges, to serve

Dipping sauce:

4 tbsp mayonnaise

2 tbsp tartar sauce

2 tbsp olive oil

1 tsp fresh lemon juice

Step 1:

Put the salmon in a large bowl. Using your hands, flake the fish into chunks.

Step 2:

Grate the potatoes into the bowl with the salmon. Stir in the egg, salt and pepper. Cover the bowl and chill for 30 minutes.

Step 3:

Thickly cover a plate with flour. Take one spoonful of the salmon mixture at a time, about the size of a golf ball.

Step 4:

Using floured hands, shape the salmon mixture to make 16 balls, then dip each of the balls in the flour until lightly coated.

Step 5: ⓘ

Heat the oil in the frying pan and fry half of the balls for 10 minutes, turning, until golden. Repeat with the remaining balls.

Step 6:

Drain the balls on paper towels. Mix together the ingredients for the sauce, then serve with the salmon balls and lemon wedges.

Marks out of 10

10=yummylicious 9=truly scrumptious 8=de-lovely
7=delicious 6=tasty 5=Mmmmmmm
4=mouthwatering 3=just nice
2=good 1=ok

. . . . ✔

Fab and Funky Kebabs★★★

Kebabs make a wicked snack at any time, but they're particularly good in the summer when they can be cooked on a barbecue. These instructions are for cooking under the grill, but they are just as yummy!

Makes 8

Prep:
15 minutes
+ 1-2 hour
marinating

Cooking:
8-10 minutes

Equipment:

- mixing bowl
- garlic crusher
- sharp knife
- chopping board
- cling film and foil
- 8 wooden skewers
- pastry brush
- tablespoon
- lemon squeezer
- slotted spoon
- plate
- tongs

What you need:

450 g boned leg of lamb
2 red onions
8 mushrooms
8 cherry tomatoes
8 bay leaves
Marinade:
4 tbsp olive oil
juice of 1 lemon
1 clove of garlic, crushed
salt and freshly ground black pepper

Step 1: ⚠️

Soak the skewers in cold water for 30 minutes. Mix together the marinade ingredients in a bowl. Cut the meat into 2 cm cubes.

Step 2:

Add the meat to the bowl and stir. Cover with cling film and leave in the fridge for 1–2 hours. Remove the meat from the bowl onto a plate.

Step 3: ⚠️

Peel the onions and cut into chunky wedges. Wash the tomatoes and wipe the mushrooms.

Step 4:

Push alternate meat cubes, onions, mushrooms, tomatoes and bay leaves onto the skewers. (Take care not to prick your fingers.)

Step 5: ⚠️

Preheat the grill. Line the grill pan with foil. Place the kebabs on the grill pan and brush with the marinade.

Step 6: ⚠️

Grill for 8–10 minutes. Turn kebabs every 2 minutes to make sure they are cooked evenly. Serve with some salad and rice, or a jacket potato.

Marks out of 10

10=yummylicious 9=truly scrumptious 8=de-lovely
7=delicious 6=tasty 5=Mmmmmmm
4=mouthwatering 3=just nice
2=good 1=ok

. . . . ✓

Jacket Potatoes★★

For a lazy evening in front of the television, hot jacket potatoes are a brilliant meal. Stuff them with your favourite fillings and eat them piping hot!

Serves 4

Prep:
15 minutes

Cooking:
75-90 minutes

Equipment:

- fork
- baking tray
- dessert spoon
- mixing bowl
- sharp knife
- chopping board
- grater

What you need:

4 large potatoes, about 250g each
55 g butter
salt and freshly ground black pepper
115 g ham
115 g Cheddar cheese

Step 1: ⓘ

Preheat the oven to 400°F/200°C/gas mark 6. Wash and wipe the potatoes. Prick with a fork and place on a baking tray.

Step 2: ⓘ

Cook the potatoes in the oven for 60–75 minutes until they are soft inside and the skins are crisp. Remove them from the oven.

Step 3:

Cut each potato in half and scoop out the soft insides into the mixing bowl. Take care not to damage the skins.

Step 4:

Mash the potato well with the fork. Add the butter and season with salt and pepper.

Step 5:

Place the skins on the baking tray. Chop the ham and put some into each shell. Spoon in the potato.

Step 6: ⓘ

Grate the cheese and sprinkle on the potatoes. Put them back in the oven and cook for a further 15 minutes until the tops are golden brown.

Marks out of 10

10=yummylicious 9=truly scrumptious 8=de-lovely
7=delicious 6=tasty 5=Mmmmmmm
4=mouthwatering 3=just nice
2=good 1=ok

. . . .

Mini Bacon and Cheese Tarts★★

Amaze your family with these mini quiches, which look fantastic when they come out of the oven all risen and golden!

Makes 6

Prep:
20 minutes
+ cooling/
chilling

Cooking:
28-33 minutes

Equipment:

- scissors
- round cutter
- deep muffin tin, 6 holes greased
- small mixing bowl
- fork
- wire cooling rack

What you need:

3 rashers lean smoked bacon
200g ready-rolled puff pastry sheet, defrosted if frozen
2 eggs, beaten
75 ml milk
55g mature Cheddar cheese, grated
1 tomato, sliced into rounds
salt and pepper
flour, for dusting

Step 1: 🛈

Heat the grill to high, then grill the bacon for 8 minutes, turning halfway through cooking. Leave to cool, then snip the bacon into small pieces using scissors.

Step 2: 🛈

Lightly flour the work surface, then place the pastry sheet on it. Use a round cutter to stamp out 6 circles large enough to fit into the holes of the muffin tin.

Step 3:

Press each pastry circle into the muffin tin. Chill for 30 minutes. Preheat the oven to 400°F/200°C/gas mark 6.

Step 4:

Sprinkle a little of the cheese and bacon into each pastry case. Put the eggs and milk in a small bowl, mix together with a fork and season with salt and pepper.

Step 5:

Pour the egg mixture into the pastry cases, filling almost to the top, then place a tomato slice on top.

Step 6: 🛈

Bake for 20–25 minutes, until risen and golden. Remove from the oven, leave the tarts to cool a little, then move to a wire rack.

Marks out of 10

10=yummylicious 9=truly scrumptious 8=de-lovely
7=delicious 6=tasty 5=Mmmmmmm
4=mouthwatering 3=just nice
2=good 1=ok

. . . .

23

Mighty Meatball Spaghetti★★★

Meatballs are always popular and these will be no exception. They come in a rich tomato sauce and are served on a bed of swirly spaghetti. Sprinkle some extra grated Parmesan cheese over the meatballs if you like.

Serves 4

Prep:
20 minutes

Cooking:
30 minutes

Equipment:

- food processor
- 2 large saucepans, one with lid
- large spoon
- colander
- garlic crusher

What you need:

1 slice crustless, day-old bread, broken into chunks
400 g lean beef mince
2 cloves garlic, crushed
1 large egg, lightly beaten
2 heaped tbsp grated Parmesan cheese
flour, for coating
300 g dried spaghetti
salt and pepper

Tomato sauce:

2 tbsp olive oil
2 cloves garlic, crushed
2 tsp dried oregano
2 x 400 g tins chopped tomatoes
1 tbsp tomato puree
1 tsp sugar

Step 1: ⚠

Put the bread in a food processor and blend until it makes breadcrumbs. Add the beef, garlic, egg, Parmesan cheese, salt and pepper.

Step 2: ⚠

Process the beef mixture until it comes together in a ball. Flour your hands and roll the mixture into balls the size of walnuts.

Step 3: ⚠

Chill the balls, then make the tomato sauce. Heat the oil in a saucepan and add the garlic and oregano. Stir for 1 minute.

Step 4: ⚠

Add the chopped tomatoes, tomato puree and sugar; bring to the boil, then reduce the heat and simmer for 8 minutes.

Step 5: ⚠

Carefully place the meatballs in the pan and spoon the sauce over them. Cover and simmer for 20 minutes, turning the meatballs occasionally.

Step 6: ⚠

Meanwhile, cook the spaghetti in a large pan of salted water, following the package instructions. Drain and serve with the meatballs and sauce.

Marks out of 10

10=yummylicious 9=truly scrumptious 8=de-lovely
7=delicious 6=tasty 5=Mmmmmmm
4=mouthwatering 3=just nice
2=good 1=ok

. . . . ✓

25

Mexican Bean Baskets★★★

A tortilla makes the perfect basket shape when baked. Put a layer of crispy shredded lettuce in the basket if you want, then top with the bean stew. A spoonful of guacamole and grated cheese taste good, too.

Serves 4

Prep:
15 minutes

Cooking:
40 minutes

Equipment:

- sharp knife
- chopping board
- large saucepan with lid
- pastry brush
- 4 heatproof bowls
- large baking tray
- garlic crusher

What you need:

2 tbsp olive oil, plus extra for brushing
2 onions, finely chopped
2 large cloves garlic, crushed
1 large red pepper, seeded and diced
2 courgettes, diced
3 tsp ground cumin
½ tsp ground cinnamon
2 tsp ground coriander
2 x 400 g tins kidney beans, drained and rinsed
2 x 400 g tins chopped tomatoes
2 tbsp ketchup
4 large, soft tortillas
salt and pepper

Step 1: ⚠️

Turn the oven on to 350°F/180°C/gas mark 4. Heat the oil in a saucepan and add the onions. Stir to coat them in the oil.

Step 2: ⚠️

Cook the onions, with the lid on, for 8 minutes, stirring now and then. Stir in the garlic, red pepper and courgettes.

Step 3: ⚠️

Next, add the spices and kidney beans, followed by the tomatoes and ketchup. Bring to a boil, then reduce the heat.

Step 4: ⚠️

Half cover the pan with a lid and simmer for 20 minutes, stirring every now and then. Season with salt and pepper.

Step 5:

Lightly brush the tortillas on both sides with oil. Place each one in a heatproof bowl, shaping the sides into a basket.

Step 6: ⚠️

Put the bowls on a baking tray and bake the tortillas for 9 minutes until crisp. Remove from the bowls. Divide the beans between the baskets.

Marks out of 10

10=yummylicious 9=truly scrumptious 8=de-lovely
7=delicious 6=tasty 5=Mmmmmmm
4=mouthwatering 3=just nice
2=good 1=ok

. . . . ✓

Crunchy Fish and Chips★★★

Wow! With this funky recipe you can make your very own take-away food at home. The fish is coated with breadcrumbs, giving it the crunchiest, crumbliest coating!

Serves 2

Prep:
25 minutes +
30 minutes
chilling

Cooking:
40-50 minutes

Equipment:

- sharp knife
- chopping board
- plate
- bowl
- fork
- shallow dish
- plastic bag
- 2 baking trays
- pastry brush
- tongs
- fish slice

What you need:

2 fillets of plaice or other white fish, skinned and cut into 1 cm-wide strips
salt and pepper
2 tbsp plain flour
1 egg
115 g white or wholemeal breadcrumbs
1 tbsp finely chopped fresh parsley
2 large potatoes, scrubbed
6 tbsp olive oil
To serve:
half a lemon, cut into segments
ketchup or mayonnaise

Step 1: (!)

Preheat the oven to 400°F/200°C/gas mark 6. Season the flour with salt and pepper and put on a plate. Roll the strips of fish in the flour until covered.

Step 2:

Beat the egg in a bowl and pour it into a shallow dish. Dip the fish into the beaten egg. Mix the parsley and breadcrumbs. Season with salt and pepper.

Step 3:

Put the mixture into a plastic bag and toss in the fish to coat thoroughly. Chill on a baking tray in the fridge for 30 minutes.

Step 4: (!)

Cut each potato into 8 wedges. Place on a baking tray and brush over half the oil. Turn the potatoes to coat them all over. Season with salt and pepper.

Step 5: (!)

Bake the chips for 35–40 minutes until golden, turning occasionally. After 20 minutes remove the fish from fridge. Drizzle with the rest of the oil.

Step 6: (!)

Bake at the top of the oven for 15-20 minutes, turning halfway through. Serve with the lemon and your favorite sauce.

Marks out of 10

10=yummylicious 9=truly scrumptious 8=de-lovely
7=delicious 6=tasty 5=Mmmmmmm
4=mouthwatering 3=just nice
2=good 1=ok

. . . . ✔

Chicken Skewers with Noodles*

Fresh, fast, and healthy, this recipe makes a perfect lunch or dinner to treat your friends and family.

Serves 4

**Prep:
20 minutes
+ marinating**

**Cooking:
15 minutes**

Equipment:

- shallow medium-size dish
- sharp knife
- chopping board
- large spoon
- cling film
- foil
- 8 wooden skewers soaked in water until ready to use
- medium saucepan
- sieve

What you need:

4 skinless chicken breasts about 150 g each, cut into 1 cm cubes
250 g medium egg noodles
2 spring onions, peeled and finely chopped
1 tbsp sesame seeds (optional)
Marinade:
4 tbsp soy sauce
2 tbsp toasted sesame oil
2 tbsp honey
5 cm piece fresh ginger, peeled and sliced
2 large cloves garlic, peeled and sliced

Step 1:

Soak the skewers in cold water for 30 minutes. For the marinade, mix all the ingredients together in a shallow dish. Add the chicken pieces and turn until coated.

Step 2:

Cover the dish with cling film. Chill, allowing the chicken to absorb the flavours of the marinade for at least 30 minutes, turning it occasionally.

Step 3: ⓘ

Preheat the grill or heat a griddle pan. Thread the chicken pieces onto 8 wooden skewers. Place in the shallow dish and spoon over a little marinade.

Step 4: ⓘ

Grill or griddle the chicken sticks for 4 minutes. Turn the sticks over, spoon over more marinade, then cook for another 4 minutes.

Step 5: ⓘ

Cook the noodles, following the package instructions. Pour the marinade through a sieve into a small pan and boil gently for 1 minute, stirring.

Step 6:

To serve, put the noodles and skewers onto 4 plates. Spoon the marinade over the noodles and sprinkle with spring onions and sesame seeds (if using).

Marks out of 10

10=yummylicious 9=truly scrumptious 8=de-lovely
7=delicious 6=tasty 5=Mmmmmmm
4=mouthwatering 3=just nice
2=good 1=ok

. . . . ✔

Sunrise Crush + Going Bananas

Bring a ray of sunshine to your day with these tropical juices that are brimming with goodness. If making juice in a blender, you may want to press it through a sieve to make it smooth.

Serves 4

Prep:
10 minutes

Cooking:
none

Equipment:

- sharp knife
- chopping board
- electric juicer, blender or food processor
- mixing bowl
- large jug
- tablespoon
- lemon squeezer

What you need:

Sunrise Crush:
1 medium ripe pineapple
5 oranges, halved
ice cubes, to serve

Going Bananas:
1 large ripe mango
4 bananas, peeled and cut into chunks
450 g plain yogurt
400 ml tin coconut milk

Sunrise Crush

Step 1: ❗
Slice the bottom off the pineapple and stand it upright on a board. Remove the spiky skin and cut into 6 pieces.

Step 2: ❗
Puree the pineapple in the electric juicer, blender or food processor.

Step 3:
Squeeze the oranges, then mix the orange and pineapple juices together in a jug. Pour the juice into 4 glasses. Top with some ice cubes.

Going Bananas

Step 1: ❗
Cut both sides of the mango away from the stone in the middle. Scoop out the flesh with a spoon.

Step 2: ❗
Slice the bananas then put in the electric juicer, blender or processor with the mango, yogurt and coconut milk.

Step 3:
Put on the lid and blend until smooth. Pour the smoothie into 4 glasses. Serve with straws.

Marks out of 10
10=yummylicious 9=truly scrumptious 8=de-lovely
7=delicious 6=tasty 5=Mmmmmmm
4=mouthwatering 3=just nice
2=good 1=ok

. . . . ✔

Fruit Smoothies*

Check out these delicious fruit smoothies, which you can mix up in minutes. Simply choose any of your favourite fruits and get creative with different mixtures to make some really zany drinks!

Serves 2

Prep:
5 minutes

Cooking:
none

Equipment:

- chopping board
- sharp knife
- teaspoon
- blender or food processor
- measuring jug

What you need:

Berry Smoothie:

1 small banana

150 g fresh raspberries and strawberries

300 ml milk

caster sugar if required

Yogurt Smoothie:

1 small banana

1 ripe pear

200 ml apple juice

200 ml natural yogurt

1 tsp vanilla extract

1 tbsp runny honey

Berry Smoothie

Step 1: (!)

For the berry smoothie, slice the banana. Halve the strawberries if they are very large.

Step 2: (!)

Place the fruit in the blender. Pour in the milk. Make sure the lid is on tight and blend until smooth.

Step 3:

Taste and add sugar if required. Pour into smoothie glasses and serve with straws.

Yogurt Smoothie

Step 1: (!)

For the yogurt smoothie, slice the banana. Peel, core and chop the pear.

Step 2: (!)

Place all the ingredients in the blender. Make sure the lid is on tight and blend until smooth.

Step 3:

Pour into smoothie glasses and serve.

Marks out of 10

10=yummylicious 9=truly scrumptious 8=de-lovely
7=delicious 6=tasty 5=Mmmmmmm
4=mouthwatering 3=just nice
2=good 1=ok

. . . .

✓

Tropical Banana Bread**

This rich, moist cake is full of fruit and is great cut into slices and packed into a lunch box. Very ripe bananas will give the best flavour.

Makes 12 slices

Prep:
25 minutes
+ cooling

Cooking:
50-60 minutes

Equipment:

- medium mixing bowl
- fork
- sieve
- large mixing bowl
- wooden spoon
- 900 g (2lb) loaf tin, greased and lined
- wire cooling rack

What you need:

5 ripe bananas (about 500g peeled weight)
200 g self-raising white flour
50 g self-raising wholemeal flour
1 tsp baking powder
125 g unsalted butter, cut into small pieces,
3 large eggs, lightly beaten
100 g golden caster sugar
100 g chopped ready-to-eat dried tropical fruit mix
icing sugar, for dusting

Step 1: ⊘
Preheat the oven to 350°F/180°C/gas mark 4. Break the bananas up into a medium bowl, then mash them with a fork until almost smooth.

Step 2:
Sift both types of flour and the baking powder into a large bowl, tipping in any bran left in the sieve. Add the butter.

Step 3:
Using your fingertips, rub the butter into the flour mixture until it looks like fine breadcrumbs.

Step 4:
Stir in the eggs, caster sugar, bananas and tropical fruit using a wooden spoon, then pour into the loaf tin.

Step 5: ⊘
Level the top using the back of the spoon, then bake for about 50–60 minutes, until risen and golden.

Step 6: ⊘
Remove from the oven and leave the cake to cool in the tin for 10 minutes. Turn out onto a wire rack. Dust with icing sugar before slicing.

Marks out of 10
10=yummylicious 9=truly scrumptious 8=de-lovely
7=delicious 6=tasty 5=Mmmmmmm
4=mouthwatering 3=just nice
2=good 1=ok

. . . .

37

Carrot Cake Squares★★

No one will ever guess that this delicious cake is made from carrots! It is one of the easiest cakes to make – no creaming or beating – but it is still light and moist with a yummy creamy topping.

Makes 16 squares

Prep: 15 minutes + cooling/ chilling

Cooking: 50 minutes

Equipment:

- sieve
- large mixing bowl
- wooden spoon
- 20 cm square cake tin, greased and lined with baking paper
- wire cooling rack
- medium mixing bowl
- palette knife
- large knife
- vegetable peeler
- grater

What you need:

110 g self-raising wholemeal flour

150 g self-raising white flour

1 tsp baking powder

2 tsp ground allspice

225 g dark brown sugar

4 medium carrots (about 250 g) peeled and grated

3 large eggs, lightly beaten

230 ml sunflower oil

Frosting:

150 g low-fat cream cheese

100 g unsalted butter, softened

1 tsp vanilla extract

300 g icing sugar

yellow, red and green ready-made icing, to decorate

Step 1: ⓘ

Preheat the oven to 350°F/180°C/gas mark 4. Sift both types of flour into a large bowl. Using a wooden spoon, stir in the baking powder, allspice, brown sugar and carrots.

Step 2:

Add the eggs and oil, then stir until mixed together. Pour the mixture into the tin and smooth the top with the back of the spoon.

Step 3: ⓘ

Bake for 50 minutes, until golden. Remove from the oven and let cool for 10 minutes, then place a wire rack on top and carefully turn out the cake.

Step 4:

When the cake is cool, beat the cream cheese, butter, vanilla extract and icing sugar in a medium bowl until smooth and creamy. Chill in the fridge for 10 minutes.

Step 5: ⓘ

Spread the frosting over the cake and smooth using a palette knife, then cut into 16 squares.

Step 6:

Mix together the yellow and red icing to make orange. Roll into 16 carrot shapes. Top each "carrot" with a small piece of green icing, then place 1 on top of each square.

Marks out of 10

10=yummylicious 9=truly scrumptious 8=de-lovely
7=delicious 6=tasty 5=Mmmmmmm
4=mouthwatering 3=just nice
2=good 1=ok

. . . . ✔

Yummy Cookies★★

These bite-sized delights are great snacks. The only problem is that everyone will love them, so don't be surprised if they all get eaten very quickly!

Makes 18

Prep:
20 minutes
+ cooling

Cooking:
15–20 minutes

Equipment:

- mixing bowl
- wooden spoon or electric hand mixer
- small bowl
- fork
- sieve
- flexible spatula
- dessert spoon
- 2 baking trays lined with baking paper
- round-bladed knife
- cooling rack
- cake tin for storage

What you need:

125 g butter

125 g golden caster sugar

1 large egg, beaten

1 ripe banana, mashed

175 g self-raising flour

1 tsp mixed spice

2 tbsp milk

100 g chocolate cut into chunks

55 g raisins

Step 1: ⓘ

Preheat the oven to 190°C/ gas mark 5. Cream together the butter and sugar with a wooden spoon or mixer until light and fluffy.

Step 2:

Add the egg gradually to the mixture, beating well each time. Mash the banana and add it in, beating until the mixture is smooth.

Step 3:

Sieve in the flour and spice. Fold in using a spatula. Add the milk to give a soft consistency. Fold in the chocolate and fruit.

Step 4:

Drop dessert spoons of the mixture onto the lined baking trays. Space cookies well apart (about 9 on each tray).

Step 5: ⓘ

Bake in the centre of the oven for 15–20 minutes until lightly golden.

Step 6: ⓘ

Remove from the oven and leave to firm up slightly. Transfer to a cooling rack using a round-bladed knife. Allow to cool before storing.

Marks out of 10

10=yummylicious 9=truly scrumptious 8=de-lovely
7=delicious 6=tasty 5=Mmmmmmm
4=mouthwatering 3=just nice
2=good 1=ok

. . . .

Very Berry Big Mess★

Nothing could be simpler to make – or more delicious to eat – than this dessert with whipped vanilla cream, fresh strawberries and chunks of chocolate cake.

Serves 4

Prep: 15 minutes

Cooking: none

Equipment:

- electric blender
- sieve
- spoon
- small and large mixing bowls
- whisk or handheld electric mixer
- wooden spoon

What you need:

450 g ripe strawberries, hulled and halved or quartered

3 tbsp icing sugar

300 ml whipping cream

2 tsp vanilla extract

4 slices chocolate sponge loaf cake or brownies

Step 1: ⓘ
Put just under half of the strawberries in a blender. Blend until pureed, then press through a sieve to remove any seeds.

Step 2:
Put the rest of the strawberries in a bowl and sprinkle over 1 tbsp of the icing sugar. Stir and set aside.

Step 3:
Pour the cream, the rest of the sugar and vanilla extract into a mixing bowl. Whisk the mixture until it forms soft peaks.

Step 4:
Break the sponge cake or brownies into large chunks and add to the cream with the strawberry puree.

Step 5:
Using a wooden spoon, gently stir the cake and strawberry puree into the whipped cream until it makes a ripple effect.

Step 6:
Spoon the cream mixture into 4 sundae dishes or bowls, then spoon over the rest of the strawberries and any juices.

Marks out of 10
10=yummylicious 9=truly scrumptious 8=de-lovely
7=delicious 6=tasty 5=Mmmmmmm
4=mouthwatering 3=just nice
2=good 1=ok

. . . . ✓

Munchy Flapjacks★★

Flapjacks are a really scrummy treat for when you have the munchies! They taste great and, as they are made from oats, they're good for you too!

Makes 18

Prep:
10-15
minutes

Cooking:
25-30
minutes

Equipment:

- rectangular 20 x 30 cm cake tin, greased and lined with baking paper
- large saucepan
- wooden spoon
- flexible spatula
- round-bladed knife
- cooling rack

What you need:

175 g butter
125 g soft light-brown sugar
55 g golden syrup
350 g porridge oats

Step 1: ⚠️

Preheat the oven to 350°F/180°C/gas mark 4. Put the butter, sugar and syrup into the saucepan.

Step 2: ⚠️

Heat pan over a low heat for 2–3 minutes, stirring until melted. Remove the pan from the hob, add the porridge oats and mix.

Step 3:

Pour the mixture into the prepared cake tin. Press down well using a spatula.

Step 4: ⚠️

Bake in the centre of the oven for 25–30 minutes until golden but still slightly soft. Remove from the oven and leave to cool for 10 minutes.

Step 5:

Cut into squares and allow to cool completely in the tin.

Step 6:

Carefully remove the flapjacks from the tin using a palette knife. Store in an airtight container for up to 1 week.

Marks out of 10

10=yummylicious 9=truly scrumptious 8=de-lovely
7=delicious 6=tasty 5=Mmmmmmm
4=mouthwatering 3=just nice
2=good 1=ok

. . . .

45

My Own Apple Pie★★★

To make your personalised apple pies, roll out the dough and carefully cut out your initials, and those of your family. After brushing the pies with egg, stick on the letters and brush again before baking.

Makes 4

Prep:
20 minutes
+ chilling

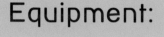

Cooking:
30-35
minutes

Equipment:

- large mixing bowl
- 4 small heatproof dishes
- rolling pin
- baking tray
- sharp knife
- cling film

What you need:

225 g plain flour
pinch of salt
2 tbsp icing sugar
125 g cold unsalted butter, cut into small pieces
1 egg, separated
1–2 tbsp cold water

Filling:
700 g apples, peeled, cored, halved and thinly sliced
2 tbsp orange juice
1 tsp ground cinnamon
3 tbsp caster sugar

Step 1:
Sieve the flour, salt and icing sugar into a bowl. Add the butter and rub it into the flour mixture with your fingertips.

Step 2:
When the mixture looks like fine breadcrumbs, mix in the egg yolk and water. Form the mixture into a ball with your hands.

Step 3:
Cover the pastry dough with cling film and chill for 30 minutes. Mix the apple slices with the orange juice, cinnamon and caster sugar.

Step 4: ⓘ
Turn on the oven to 400°F/200°C. Divide the apple mixture between the 4 heatproof dishes. Wet the rim of each dish.

Step 5: ⓘ
Roll out the pastry dough and cut 4 round tops. Top each pie with a pastry circle, trim the edges, and press with a fork.

Step 6: ⓘ
Brush the tops with egg white and make a slit in them. Decorate as shown on the opposite page. Put on a baking tray and bake for 30–35 minutes.

Marks out of 10
10=yummylicious 9=truly scrumptious 8=de-lovely
7=delicious 6=tasty 5=Mmmmmmm
4=mouthwatering 3=just nice
2=good 1=ok

. . . .

✓

How To...

Here are some useful cooking words and terms:

Grate cheese

Hold the cheese against a grater and rub it up and down over the large holes to make coarse shreds — keep your fingers out of the way.

Separate eggs

Crack the egg, pull open the shell with your fingers, and let it plop into a bowl. Put an egg cup over the yolk and pour the white into another bowl.

Rub in

When making pastry, mix or rub the butter into the flour with your fingertips until the mixture resembles fine bread crumbs.

Roll out dough

Lightly flour the surface and rolling pin, then roll out the dough away from you in gentle movements, turning it occasionally, until it makes a thin sheet.

Whip

To add air to cream or egg whites, beat them with a whisk until they firm up and form peaks.

Cream

To add air to cakes, beat the butter and sugar together with a whisk or wooden spoon until they are light and creamy in texture.

Melt chocolate

Put the bowl of chocolate pieces over a pan of gently simmering water until melted. Make sure the bowl does not touch the water.

Cook pasta/noodles

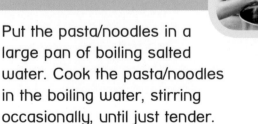

Put the pasta/noodles in a large pan of boiling salted water. Cook the pasta/noodles in the boiling water, stirring occasionally, until just tender.